Snip-Snap, Clickety-Click!

Written by Joëlle Murphy
Illustrated by Keiko Narahashi

Celebration Press
An Imprint of Pearson Learning

MY PHOTO
ALBUM

Snip-snap, clickety-click.

It's a cloudy day.

Snip-snap, clickety-click.

It's a windy day.

Snip-snap, clickety-click.
It's a rainy day.

5

Snip-snap, clickety-click.

It's a snowy day.

Snip-snap, clickety-click.
It's a sunny day.

Snip-snap, clickety-click.
That's me at the beach!